Believe Cleave Receive Achieve

Believe Cleave Receive Achieve

Debra Butler

Believe Cleave Recieve Achieve

Republished by Redemption Press 2017

Published by Redemption Press,
PO Box 427, Enumclaw, WA 98022
Toll Free (844) 2REDEEM (273-3336)

Redemption Press is honored to present this title in partnership with the author. The views expressed or implied in this work are those of the author. Redemption Press provides our imprint seal representing design excellence, creative content, and high quality production.

ISBN: 978-1-68314-694-0

Mary Noorjian

Midlands Prop

1016 W Confederate
MidlandsPro
803

DONALD A. JOYNER JR.
603 CRYSTAL ANNE LN
ROANOKE, VA 24019

Dear Mr. Joyner,

First, allow me to take a moment to offer m
one, Donald Joyner Sr. It is often the case
to pay taxes, pay any outstanding liabilities
interested in selling the property for these o

Often, I buy real estate and other personal p
understanding that your loved one left prop
I would be interested in making you an offe

Some of the advantages I may be able to

- You need make no repairs. I will bu

This book is dedicated to God
the Father, The Son and The Holy Spirit.

I thank God along with everyone
who helped me become who
I am today.

We all want a good life. We all want to feel happiness and joy and God wants to give that to us.

The promises He made, like God Himself, will never change. Those promises are a good life lived with joy, and love, without fear, worry, or anxiety. We all have troubles and tribulations, God promised we'd have those as well but with Him we can face them trusting God. We must believe first in order to receive His blessings.

We can receive God's promises by keeping Him first in our lives. When we put God first everything else falls into place perfectly, exceeding anything we could plan for ourselves.

From my first memories, I was talking to God. I'd play and sing songs with rhymes all day long, nurturing the gift the Holy Spirit gave me to write poetry. When I first used my gift for God's glory I wrote "Your Love" and they kept coming. Sometimes I would get a single thought or story, or idea and once I got that, it was almost as if something took over and I was simply listening.

When I went through a trial, God spoke to my heart and told me if I jumped off the boat He could save me but not until then. With a lot of faith, I took that step and poured myself into God and the Gospels and out of them came another dozen poems bringing life to words written thousands of years ago.

We are living in a generation of prophesy being played out before our eyes. Now is the time to secure your connection with God and His awesome power.

Through my trial, I had that peace that cannot be explained. And He carried me to the place I am now. When my world should have been shaken to its core, God took over. I allowed myself to be still and quiet so that God could work His miracles. One day I was in the trial and then, I am not sure how, I am relocated near family and my only child, living out my dream to live near the ocean.

Jesus performed more miracles on Earth than can be recorded and said over and over "Your faith has healed you". I believe FAITH stands for "Feeling As If That's Happened". If we pray with faith, knowing and feeling as we would when our prayers are answered, fix our minds on them being answered, then we open ourselves to all kinds of blessings. Knowing you're blessed is the first step to more blessings. Expecting them is the second. We must first Believe and Cleave to our God not letting go, joining ourselves to Him, and then we can Receive His blessings and Achieve our goals!

Every one of the thousands of thoughts that go through our heads every day bring about a feeling. We control those thoughts; we can immediately reject a thought that makes us feel bad or we can dwell on it adding fuel to the fire. This is exactly what the enemy wants, why he put the thought in your head in the first place. He wants us to feel bad, unworthy. We need to learn to immediately push that thought out and replace it with the thought that we are children of God and as His children He wants the best things in life for us. If we dwell on that, more things will come to us to back that belief up. He has the awesome power to make things happen. Our connection with God is more important than any other in our lives.

The poems in this book reflect my personal relationship and love for God and The Word as contained in the Bible. He said, "If you draw close to me I will stay near you". Let yourself feel the love of God knowing He loves you as if you were the only person in the world. And, let yourself be reminded of His promises. God bless you.

Contents

You Are My Rock

You are the rock that I'm anchored to.
You watch and see everything I go through.
You know my love for you is strong and true,
Despite some of the things I say and do.

You love me still, though I'm weak and frail.
Even when I'm tested and clearly fail.
When holding my breath, you help me exhale,
Get me back on my feet and you help me prevail.

You are my rock, my strength on which I rely.
You open my wings while you teach me to fly.
Don't let me go; I'm getting closer to the sky.
Hold my wings open, Lord, bring me up high.

You are my rock, my truth, and my light.
I want to fly with you with all of my might.
Please, Lord, don't let me out of your sight.
Stay with me, and I will surely win this fight.

The Promise

And suddenly right before my eyes,
after all of the pain,
My heart still breaking
knowing it would never be the same.
My tears still stinging,
my tears falling like rain,
There He stood, larger than life,
I had Him back again.

I listened to all His stories,
I loved listening to Him speak.
He made me feel I could do anything,
without Him I was weak.
I wanted to embrace Him,
never let Him out of my sight,
I knew that with Him beside me
I'd never have to fear the night.

How can I explain the joy
of having Him back again?
My spirit was lifted, my broken heart,
my heart began to mend.
I never thought I'd ever again
lay eyes upon my friend,
After knowing how He had suffered
right to the bitter end.

And then He made a promise,
He said, "I will always be near,
Though your eyes may not see me
you have nothing to fear,
And when the weight on your shoulders
seems too much to bear,
Call my name, believe this promise,
your voice I will hear."

What Matters

How could she just sit there with everything going on?
By the time I take care of everything He will be gone.
I have to prepare a meal and serve the guests in my home,
And there she sits leaving me to do everything alone.

I have so many things to worry about and she doesn't care.
She's anointing His feet and wiping them with her hair.
And He says,
"Martha, why do you worry about meaningless things?
Your sister has chosen to do what matters
for the joy that it brings."

And when He came back
after my brother Lazarus had died;
I told Him He could have come back sooner
and saved him if He tried.
And He said,

"Your brother shall rise; I will bring him forth today,
I am the life and resurrection
and whoever believes will be saved."

Jesus went to the tomb
and asked that they clear away the stone,
And He spoke to His Father
to show He didn't do this alone.
And He thanked God for hearing Him
and called Lazarus' name.
And from the tomb,
though dead for days,
my brother lived again.

There was no question
but that He was the Christ sent from above,
To show us there is no need to worry
if we trust in God's love.
And I learned it doesn't matter
how the rest of the world sees us;
All that matters
is the time we spend
at the feet of Jesus.

Luke 10:38-42
John 11:1-44

The Door

Stop long enough until you can hear it and then listen
To the voice deep inside that you so often ignore.
It's there to help you to make the right choices
And take you higher than you've ever been before.

Just be still and listen, and let the voice take you
To that higher place, and don't be afraid to soar.
It's all about living and growing and learning
To recognize the voice that will let you be sure.

Stay tuned to that voice, and know when it speaks;
It will tenderly nudge you or it will wage a war.
It will battle the will of your weak human spirit.
Don't question where it will lead; dare to explore.

It will lead you to places you've never dreamed of before
Like the kingdom of Heaven that's just through the door.
Follow the voice of the Lord; He's what you're longing for.
Through the door is your treasure and you'll search no more.

The Man You Think I Am

He said I wish I could be the man that you think I am.
My confidence says I can't but you believe I can.
I know that I am not half the man you had in your plan,
When you formed me out of nothing and my life began.

He says I want to be what you have created me to be.
I want to walk in your light and do what is right,
Know how to reject evil when it tries to tempt me,
And be strengthened by your love, power and might.

I want to not be affected by the world and its ways;
It promises you happiness then it takes it away.
You are always there through even my darkest days.
Your promises are real I know that each time I pray.

I want to look in the mirror and see the man that you see;
The one who has been set free to be all that I can be.
I want to do all those things you have planned for me,
Resist evil, remain free, live my life more abundantly.

I Wish...

I wish I could have known you
when you walked upon this earth.
I wish I could have been there
to praise your blessed birth.
I wish I could have been with you
when you were just a boy,
Kissed by God, His beloved Son,
filled with heavenly joy.

I wish I could have been there
when you fed your hungry lambs,
With holy bread and holy fish
granted at your command.
I wish I could have been there
when you calmed the mighty sea
And ruled all of nature
with such grand authority.

I wish I could have watched you
as you overpowered death,
And filled the lungs of Lazarus
with your own eternal breath.
I wish I could have seen you
heal the blind, the deaf, the lame,
And watched them leap and sing with joy
and praise your blessed name.

I wish I could have seen your glory
as you rose from the dead,
And moved the stone and left your tomb
to rise and live instead.
I wish I could have heard your angels
and had the courage to sing.
Yes, I will praise your name forever, Lord!
Blessed be Our King!

Unchained

Not even the raging storm could do anything but obey
when we thought our boat could take no more.
In an instant the storm ended at His word
and the waves that tossed us now helped us to shore.
And at once a madman with an unclean spirit
naked and scarred came running towards Jesus.
Falling at His feet he cried "Son of the Most High,
it is not our time, don't torture us, please leave us."

They knew Him in Heaven, before being cast out,
before their desire to put themselves above Him.
Their pride drove them away to torture the souls
of those who would otherwise love Him.
They always cry out when they see Him,
begging this not be the end, falling to the ground.
"If you cast us out, send us into the swine"
and into the lake they ran where each one was drowned.

Those watching told the people in the city
about the demon-possessed man they had to bind,
They came and saw the man at the feet of Jesus,
he was clothed, healed and in his right mind.
Then their fear sent us away,
the saved man pleaded to stay;
there was nothing he could do.
Jesus said, 'Go home and tell everyone
what God has done,
about the mercy He had on you'.

Though he longed to stay he went back home,
and told of the great things the Lord had done.
He said Jesus has saved me from a legion of demons;
so you could see His forgiveness is for everyone.
The glory of God was seen through this man's salvation,
his healing and his freedom from sin.
And the people's fear was replaced with faith in God;
and they put their love and trust in Him.

Luke 8:22-39

Double Miracle

I was a well-respected ruler in the temple;
there's so much that money can't buy.
My only child was sick, my position could do nothing,
it was hard for me to realize.

I heard the crowd outside, Jesus was coming,
my baby was fading right before my eyes.
I made my way through the crowd thinking,
I must get to Him before my child dies.

This huge crowd was unruly;
they were waiting for Him to pull His boat to shore.
The multitude allowed me through,
they knew who I was by the clothes I wore.

I fell at His feet, "My daughter is dying,
she is only twelve," I began to implore,
I knew that if He could touch her she would live;
she would be healed for sure.

We moved through the crowd
and suddenly He stopped, I thought this cannot be;
He said, 'Who touched my clothes?', and waited,
Again, He asked, "Who touched me?"

There were so many people crowding against Him,
He was wasting time why didn't He see.
Having no choice, a woman stepped forward,
trying to go unnoticed she said, "It was me".

"I have been sick for twelve years, no one could help me,
I was weak, I fought to get to you.
I knew if I could touch the edge of your cloak
you would cure me you would make me new.

"At that very moment I felt my strength return
and I knew I had been saved by you!"
He knew only great faith could take His power and said,
"Daughter, go in peace, your faith has healed you".

A messenger came and told me not to bother Jesus
my little girl had died but He stayed.
Ignoring the message, He told me
she will be healed just believe and do not be afraid.

The mourners laughed when He said she's sleeping,
we went inside where she laid.
He took her by the hand and gave a command,
He said "*Arise*" and even death obeyed.

It was a miracle! He put His hands on my child
and she lived when she was dead!
The mourners would be amazed
but He ordered us
'Nothing about this is to be said.'

He took the time with a faithful woman
who had been living a life of dread.
I asked Jesus to heal my daughter
but He chose to wait
and resurrect her instead!

Luke 8:40-56

Second Chances

Where would any of us be
without second chances;
And a hundred second chances
after that?
We all start at the gate
with the whole world before us;
And sometimes we don't all make it back.

It's the second chance
that will bring you home,
No matter how many times
you get off track.
God's love for you is strong.
You will never be alone;
Your second chance will always bring you back.

Prayer

No matter how many times I see it,
No matter how many times I'm shown,
The power of prayer is greater
Than any other I've ever known.
"Ask and you shall receive"
Seems too simple to be true.
Still, no matter what I ask for,
There's nothing He can't do.

Faith is all it takes.
Pray with faith and it's yours.
When there seems no way out
He will open all the doors.
Believe in what you ask for;
Ask it in His name.
Once you see what happens
Your life will never be the same.

Prayer is the key to life.
Life without prayer leaves you cold.
Unite your life with God.
Allow His love to make you bold.
He has always been here,
And He is always the same.
He is eager to grant you
What you ask for in His name.

No matter how many times
You get an answer to your prayers,
It will continue to astonish you
When you see how much He cares.
Pray every day with faith and love.
There's nothing God can't do.
It's a very precious thing to Him,
A prayer filled with faith from you.

Draw From His Love

He in heaven who made us loves us as only He can.
With a depth of love no mortal mind
could truly understand.
But a love which was in existence before time began
Is what we need to draw from today
as we strive to live His command.

He in heaven who loves us is with us
through all of our days.
Even as we fall into temptation,
our Savior in Heaven prays
That we will draw from His love
and seek His mercy that saves.
We just need to call on His name,
love Him and honor Him with praise.

He in Heaven loves us
no matter where we might have been.
It's never too late to draw from His love
and start over again.
We must have faith in His forgiveness
and forgive all other men;
And truly believe His love will heal us
and free us from sin.

His mercy can open any lock
but we must walk through the door,
Confess our sin, and allow Him to cleanse us
and make our hearts pure.
We just need to call on His name
and our place in Heaven is assured
As long as we learn to obey Him
and love Him and know that Jesus is Lord.

End Your Search

When the road you're walking on
feels like an uphill climb,
And the load you're made to carry
gets heavier all the time,
You search for the solution
that will help support the weight.
The more questions you think you answer
the more you create.

You may search for your entire life
and never find relief
From the load you're made to carry
bringing only grief.
The world is full of people
who will promise you a cure
If you only invest in their ideas,
they promise to sell you more.

It won't be long before new burdens
are added to the weight
And the promises made by people
no longer seem that great.
And you begin to believe this hardship
has somehow become your fate.
You stop searching for the solution
as you're certain it's too late.

Other people cannot help you;
they're not equipped for the role.
They're just as lost as you are
on their journey toward their goal.
There's only one source available
that will truly make you whole;
The answers you've been searching for
are deep within your soul.

Think about giving Jesus a chance
to fulfill the promises He made.
He promised He would hear you
and answer every time you prayed.
He already knows your needs and loves you
even if you've strayed.
Your soul is longing to unite with God
whose love will never fade.

Jesus promised He'd take our burdens,
our grief, and our pain.
He promised he would give us
what we asked for in His Name.
He promised that with faith
our lives would never be the same.
End your search with Jesus
let Him help you with your strain.
End your search with Jesus
you have everything to gain.

Tough People Do

When it's all over you remember tough times don't last.
Even in the eye of the storm remember this too shall pass.
And no matter what this time may be putting you through,
Never forget that tough times don't last, tough people do!

When the storm seems stronger than what you can endure,
And it feels never ending like you can't take anymore,
Face the storm you're in
with the strength of God at your side,
With His strength and your faith, you will turn any tide.

No matter how violent the storm God is stronger still,
And when the next storm rages as you know it will,
Remember, that tough times don't last, tough people do;
Fear not for God will get you through this one too.

Get Up And Walk

Pick up your mat and walk!
Don't just talk the talk.
No matter where you are right now,
Pick up your mat and walk somehow.

The power is within you,
Incredible things you can do.
You're never too low don't ever let go,
Get off your mat and let the healing flow.

Stand up and let your faith heal you.
Let all those around feel you.
The grace that has brought you to your feet
Will be felt in some way by everyone you meet.

You have lives to change by your own story.
You were born to live boldly for His glory.
God's healing mercy will lift you to your feet;
He will lift you to victory in the midst of defeat.

Pick up your mat and walk!
Stop complaining it's only talk.
Do something instead inside your own head,
Forgive yourself for the things you've done and said.

You have the power that God gave to you
To do all the things you need to do.
You are forgiven but you need to move on;
And take those chances before they're all gone!

Abundant Harvest of a Rich Man

Pulling up in his new sports car
he is proud of his success.
He thought his hard work and dedication
provided his excess.
His cup was running over, he thought I deserve the best.
Others don't work as hard as me that's why they have less.

He pulled into his triple garage thinking
I will need more space.
Entering his mansion, he thought I'll need a bigger place.
Sitting back in his chair he could finally slow the pace.
He had more than enough to get through
anything he faced.

And suddenly without warning
He breathed his last breath and died.
No one got to appreciate
what he had stored for himself inside.

So much he could have given
to those less fortunate if he tried.
He could have saved his own life
if he had shared what God supplied.

Luke 12:16-21

Fear Nothing But Fear Itself

God asked me to stand up for righteousness sake.
He said I have laid kings and princes at your feet.
He said the good land is here, yours to take.
I will help you through any obstacles you meet.

I did this and He was bringing me to the good land.
Encouraged was I to face my enemy and win.
God was watching over me I was in the Lord's hand.
He said stand up for me and show the enemy their sin.

I was to take that land with faith and bravery.
God laid the land before me and said this is yours.
He gave me the courage to be all I had to be,
And He was bringing me safely to the shore.

Without warning I allowed fear to enter my heart.
Satan was standing up for the wicked against me.
My faith was shaken, the devil would not depart.
I no longer had the courage to be what I had to be.

Fear would not allow me to enter the good land.
God was handing it to me but fear got in the way.
I was not able to follow through as God had planned.
And the good land that was offered me was taken away.

Day After Day

"Just let me go back for a minute", the rich man said,
So that I can warn my family of what lies ahead.
I'm sure they'd do things differently if they only knew
That you're paid back for everything
you did and didn't do.

I would have cared for Lazarus
who begged outside my door.
He was always there, a nuisance, he became an eye sore.
Day after day he'd lie outside
my beautiful mansion pleading,
And day after day
I'd walk right by ignoring his needing.

I had wonderful garments, I had riches beyond compare,
And now I find myself in this awful place I can't bear.
Lazarus had nothing, no clothes, no pride, no charms.
And now I see him day after day
cradled in Abraham's arms.

"He who possessed nothing
is now in the presence of God above.
His wounds are healed, he's fed,
he no longer hungers for love.
And I had everything, the best;
I wouldn't settle for any less,
And now I'm naked, cold, and alone in this wilderness.

"Just let me go back to warn the rest of my family
of what's to be.
I could save them from this place if they could just see me."
But he was told that he was told so many times
in many ways
That the compassion you show others
comes back to you one day.
So care for those you meet,
greet everyone with love and respect.
You may not think it makes a difference
but it has a huge effect
On where you will spend your time
when you are no longer here.
Humble yourself, lose your pride,
and the rest will become clear.

Luke 16:19-31

Mercy

Assuming I could trip Him up,
"For eternal life", I asked, "what must I do?"
He turned and asked me,
"What is written in the law?
What is asked of you?"

"Love your neighbor as yourself.
and God with a love that's strong and true"
He said, "You have answered correctly."
I was testing Him, it was like He knew.

"And who is my neighbor?" I had Him now,
He couldn't escape my prying.
"A man was stripped, robbed and beaten"
was the way he was replying,
"A priest saw him but he crossed the street
and left the beaten man dying.
A Levite came by and thought
I can't help this man I'm not even trying."

"But mercy was found in a Samaritan who stopped
and cared for his injuries.
He brought him on his own donkey to an innkeeper
and paid for all the fees.
He said, "I will pay what I owe when I come back
just take care of him please".
Jesus testing me asked,
"Who was this man's neighbor, out of these three?"

I thought I could trip Him up,
how could no one trap Him, not even me?
I was a shrewd lawyer
but I found myself with no choice but to agree.
I was lured by Jesus to answer by saying,
"It was the one who showed mercy".
He used my questions to teach the people
that our neighbor is everyone we see.

Luke 10:25-37

The Division

There will be no doubt
when Jesus comes with all His glory.
The whole world will know at once and stand before thee.
He will sit upon His thrown with all His angels at His side.
The world will stand in judgment
and He will start to divide.

As a watchful shepherd separates the goats from the sheep,
The goats will go to the left, the sheep on the right to keep.
And then the king will say to those he put on his right
"Come you who are blessed by my Father into the light."

"The kingdom prepared
since the beginning of time is for you.
You fed me and clothed me
there was nothing you wouldn't do."
The righteous will say "Lord when did we do these things?"
He will answer,
"When you did it for the least you did it for The king."

And to those on His left He will order
"You are cursed depart from me.
"The hungry, the homeless, the thirsty,
you chose not to see;
"And when you refused to help them
you refused to help me."
They will go to eternal punishment
but the righteous to life eternally!

Standing Strong With God

Have great faith in the Lord your God
and all He has in store for you.
His love is like that of a loving father,
there's nothing He wouldn't do.
For those He has chosen to call His own,
He can make you like new.
And with His love and His strength
there's nothing you can't do.

Live in this truth and believe it is true
every day with all your heart.
And the blessings you receive from God
will be way off the chart.
There's nothing in this world
that could tear you and God apart.
The power He has given you
has been yours right from the start.

God has given you power to stand strong
against any evil force before you.
He has given you authority to overcome the enemy
in everything you do.
And He will give you the courage you need
when you fight for what is true.
Stand firm in that faith knowing
that this power is there for you.

Do not be afraid for God will always provide
to those who believe it is so.
Even as you face your trials
you can face them with trust and always know
That God will bring you through
and through it your faith will grow;
And you can remain strong without fear
knowing God will never let you go.

He is Found

Jesus was again speaking to the Scribes and Pharisees
Of a man with two sons and how both held the keys.
The younger son asked for his portion now
and he went away
To a far country, far from his father
was where he would stay.

He lost what was given to him by his father,
he threw it away.
Left with nothing he went to work in a pig sty to
have somewhere to stay.
Willing to eat the pods fed to the pigs
he came to his senses one day.
'I have sinned against you treat me as a servant',
that's what I'll say.

But his father had been waiting for him
And when he saw him come near
He ran to him and kissed him
and ordered the servants,
"Bring a robe here."

He confessed his sin,
"I am no longer worthy to be called your son, I fear".
But his father said,
"My son was lost but he's found!
Give him a ring to wear".

When the older son heard the celebration
he refused to attend.
He told his father I have served you,
your commands I never tried to bend.
My brother gets a feast;
he spent everything on every kind of sin.
His father said, "Your brother was dead,
we celebrate because he lives again!"

Luke 15:11-32

There Is a Kingdom

More magnificent than the golden red of a sunset in July;
More brilliant than the crystal blue of a clear autumn sky;
More intense than the blaze of the
constant rays of the sun;
The place from where time began
can be compared to none.

The eyes we've been given
have beheld nothing quite like this.
If you never experience pure perfection,
it will never be missed.
The golden reds of a sunset
and the bright blue hue of the sky
Will produce a sense of satisfaction,
of perfection to your eye.

There is a Kingdom that exists
with no limits of time or space.
Its magnificence cannot be explained,
interpreted, or erased.
There is a Kingdom where you can look
upon God's holy face;
Where you can hear the voice of an angel,
there is such a place.

More love than the most caring mother
could have ever shown.
More kindness, peace, and harmony
than you or I have ever known.
More comfort and compassion
where you will never feel alone.
There is a Kingdom that waits
for those who God calls His own.

Take Time to Praise

Give praise to the Father in everything you do.
His power is all-consuming; His unending love is true.
He deserves your praise; He makes everything new.
He battles evil every moment; He's fighting for you.

Give praise to the Father before beginning your day;
Before your troubles take over, make time to pray.
He's waiting for you; it doesn't matter what you say;
The words will come to you; praise Him today.

Give praise to the Son; He deserves it as well.
He left the world He knew to save those who fell.
He called those who would listen; He had stories to tell
Of the kingdom of Heaven and a place called Hell.

All those that would listen were saved by His grace.
He's still saving the souls of those in His embrace.
He longs to save you. Don't lose sight of His face;
And He will give you the strength to finish the race.

Give praise to the Holy Spirit of God up above;
Who gave praise to the Son in the form of a dove.
With the Father and Son, He forms the trinity of love.
He's the comforter, the Spirit of God Jesus spoke of.

Take time to speak to the Spirit, the Father, and the Son.
Cherish the knowledge that they love you as no other one.
They long to feel your love before your time here is done.
Give thanks and praise and your victory will be won.

The Edge

There he sits on the edge of his bed
with a gun to his head
Wondering if he'd be better off dead.
The dread is overtaking him; he tries so hard to find
Something good in his life,
wishing he could stop the rewind.

There is nothing left but hopelessness and regret.
He is too close to the edge; his soul is too far in debt.
He stares into space. The only color he sees is gray.
His world is black and white. He can't face another day.

How did this happen to him? Where did he go wrong?
He was on top of the world looking lean and strong.
But the world was on top of him; he was under the weight;
Of regret for the things that have brought him to this fate.

There he sits on the edge of his bed
with a gun to his head
Wondering where those other paths might have lead.
Now his soul is a wasteland; empty except for hate
For himself and his actions and he's sure it's too late.

He drops the gun to the floor and holds his head and cries
For all the heartbreak he has caused, and again he tries
To remember the reason why he should live another day
But he can't find one; it's so painful watching the replay.

Even in this hour, God the Father watches from above,
Praying that he remembers the only reason is love.
Not that he loves God but that God loved him
Enough to go out on a limb to take away his sin.

And God loves him even as he sits on the edge of his bed.
Like a loving father, He longs to take away all the dread.
His debt has been paid; his soul is free from sin.
God prays now that His child will call on Him.

On The Third Day

Early in the morning on the first day of the week
before the sun broke through the night,
God's word fulfilled, Jesus had risen from the dead,
guards trembling at the sight.
Angels mighty and powerful are at the tomb now
and they are praising God with all their might.
They're waiting for Mary who was saved by Jesus,
who was at the cross, who never left His side.

Through the darkness, as she got closer,
she could see the tomb was covered no more.
The stone was moved so she could look inside
and it was empty of that she was sure.
She ran to the disciples who were still grieving
over the suffering and death of their lord.
"The rock's been moved the tomb is empty,
Jesus isn't in there anymore."

"Come see!" she said, and they took off running
John then Peter and Mary behind.
When they reached the tomb, Peter went inside
not sure of what he would find.
There lay the strips of linen undisturbed
where the Lord's lifeless body had reclined,
They were not unwrapped,
His body left the linen,
there was nothing left to bind.

John stepped in and saw the napkin
that covered His battered face neatly folded off to the side.
Jesus made a statement by folding the napkin;
they could not keep Him dead, although they tried.
They left confused but after seeing,
John remembered what Jesus told them before He died.
He was the first to believe but Mary was still grieving,
she stood outside the tomb and cried.

Still crying she bent down and looked inside the tomb
as she heard someone say,
"Why are you crying?"
She saw two angels inside then said,
"They have taken my Lord away,"
She turned and saw who she thought was the gardener
and said, "Tell me where He is I beg"
He said, "*Mary*".
She was the first to see Him,
And the darkness gave way to the day.

John 20:1-16

Today

Open your eyes to a brand new day.
Let yesterday's troubles fade away.
Tomorrow is another whole day away.
Live in the wonder and splendor of today!

This is a gift, you see, another day.
A gift for you to do with as you may.
Disappointment will only waste it away.
Don't spend it reliving yesterday.

Wrap both arms around this brand new day.
Embrace the new opportunities on their way.
Don't let God's gift to you slip away.
Live every moment to the fullest today.

May's Glory

It happens in an instant; in an instant a life can change,
And all the things you know somehow become strange.
Those things that were so important just the day before.
Become nothing in that instant;
they don't matter anymore.

We watched you with such admiration, love, and fear.
As you walked through that door you left us all here.
And we prayed and we loved you
and we prayed some more;
That you'd come back to us stronger than before.

With every step you had to take we were there at your side
Keeping you strong in our love, a love we cannot hide.
We sent our cards and our meals that were made with care.
Even though you couldn't see us
we were somehow always there.

And then our prayers were answered
and you came back home
To the people who love you like you were their very own.
It's a family we've created and it's rare today, we're told,
But all we cared about was that you came back to the fold.

Your family and friends thought
of all the reasons they cared.
They brought to mind
all the wonderful things they shared
With someone who means so much in so many ways.
You will remain a part of us all for the rest of our days.

The King's Feast

The invites were sent by the king a long time ago;
at last the feast was set.
There was gold, fine linens,
the choicest foods, his son deserved the best.

He sent his servants to bring the guests
to the long-awaited wedding fest.
But instead they mistreated some of his servants,
and others killed the rest.

The king became enraged and sent his troops,
his wrath had been renown.
He ordered them to be destroyed
and he burned their city down.

They were undeserving to attend the feast
and so the king looked around
And asked his servants to go out again
and invite everyone they found.

There were good and bad alike,
the palace was completely filled with guests.
They were eating and drinking
for the first time in their lives they had all the best.

When the king saw a certain man
he asked how he had gotten in with the rest.
The man was silent, he could not stay
because of the way that he was dressed.

The king ordered he be bound by his hands and feet
and thrown into the night;
To suffer and cry and gnash his teeth
because his repentant heart was not right.

And He said the Kingdom of God is much like this
and it is right before your sight.
Make straight your path, make pure
your heart and remain within His light.

A Promise Fulfilled

God promised a savior, the Messiah, to Abraham
And to his sons Isaac and Jacob and their sons.
Generation to generation to King David's reign
To the exile and beyond they waited for the one.

Generations of oppression had come and gone
They remembered the hope, the promise made.
From Solomon to the deportation into Babylon,
For their king, their savior, the messiah they prayed.

Another fourteen generations and Jacob had a son.
His name was Joseph, he grew to be a righteous man,
He was betrothed to Mary, he knew she was the one.
God chose obedient Mary, a virgin, to fulfil His plan.

Before they were united Mary was found to be with child.
From the Holy Spirit the child of God was conceived.
Joseph felt betrayed and those around her were riled,
They found Mary's story one that couldn't be believed.

He thought he'd divorce her quietly saving her from shame.
As he considered this an angel appeared to him in a dream.
The angel said "Joseph, son of David, it is as Mary claims,
The child she carries
is the hope of all people to be redeemed."

"This child is from the Holy Spirit
and Jesus will be His name.
He will save His people from their sins,
take Mary, all is well."
These things took place to fulfill
what the prophet had proclaimed,
"The virgin will bear a son
and they shall call him Emmanuel".

When Joseph arose
he did as the angel had commanded him.
Through his obedience he accepted Jesus
into his life as his son.
All who trust in Jesus Christ can receive
forgiveness of their sins.
This promise made generations ago can never be undone.

Matthew 1:1-25

The Perfect Gift

I've read the laws as received by Moses
And learned the penalty that sin imposes.
For sinners, the door to God always closes;
And we all fall short according to Moses.

Salvation appeared impossible for anyone,
With God's laws, it seemed it couldn't be done.
Salvation was lost when time had first begun;
When Adam and Eve put their trust in the evil one.

There is no hope for us in this world on our own.
And with no hope of salvation we can never atone,
But there's wonderful news: we're no longer alone.
God sent His Son to love us and bring us back home.

We've done nothing to deserve salvation, even to this day.
It's a priceless gift from our Father we could never repay.
The only blameless one died in order to show us the way.
His blood paid for our sins;
Remember that when you pray.

Recall the laws God set in place thousands of years ago.
Obey those laws with all your might
and let everybody know;
That salvation is possible
if you believe in Jesus and never let go
Of the promise He made of eternal life
For those who believe it is so.

Song to Peter

Empty nets were all you had to show
after being on Lake Gennesaret all night.
You struggle to bring your boat to shore,
when something peculiar catches your sight.

It's a man speaking to thousands of people
Who are clinging to His every word.
They push Him to the water's edge.
He boards your boat, and your heart is stirred.

After His sermon, He asked that you pull your boat out
and cast your nets again.
You tell Him there were no fish all night.
He promised He'd make you a fisher of men.

You drop your nets, and as soon as you do,
they are tearing from the strain.
You filled two boats with the fish you caught,
and you never looked back again.

It was you who walked on the water with Him.
What a miraculous thing to do.
You doubted; you sank and cried,
"Save me, Jesus!" and you were the first who knew.

When asked what people say of Him,
it was you who confessed He was the Son of Man.
He blessed you, Simon, and named you Peter,
the rock, on whom His church would stand.

Salt of the earth, light of the world,
you were sent among wolves to preach His word.
You showed them signs they'd never seen,
taught them things they'd never heard.

How you begged Him not to return to Jerusalem
where He told you He would die.
And it was you who saw Him being led away
and all three times you would deny.

Oh, Peter, how your heart must have ached
for having denied knowing the King of kings,
But He knew you were grieving.
He knew how you loved Him;
He knew all these things.

And how your heart must have been lifted up
when you visited the tomb of the Son of Man;
And found an angel where the Lord had been
who told you of the fulfillment of God's plan.

Never again would your nets be empty;
you filled them with believers again and again.
The very Spirit of Jesus was within your soul
as you preached His victory over sin.

Faith provided strength to fight the good fight
and you fought for Christ to the end.
You devoted your life to the Lord and His people
and you truly became God's fisher of men.

Times Like These

It's times like these when I'm so at ease.
Everything's right, and life's a breeze.
That's when I stop and get on my knees,
And say thank you Jesus for times like these.

You make these times that are so right.
Life's a joy and the future's bright.
That's when I pray with all my might
That you'll always keep me in your sight.

And I pray that you'll hear me when I say,
I love you, Jesus, bless your children today.
It's times like these when it's going my way
That I thank you Jesus all night and day.

One Sabbath Day

The people loved Jesus, they came to find Him every day.
The synagogue leaders kept trying to keep Him away.
A crippled woman sat in the synagogue one Sabbath day;
As Jesus taught she thought
For eighteen years I've been this way.

Knowing her thoughts
He called her forward for everyone to see.
He said, "You've been crippled by a spirit
but today you are set free."
He put His hands on her
and she stood up straight immediately!
She went away praising God saying,
"Look how Jesus healed me!"

The leaders were jealous of Jesus,
He was known by everyone.
Thousands came to Him,
no matter where He was, they'd come.
The leaders told the people,
"There are six days for work to be done,
No one is to work on a Sabbath day,
she could be healed on another one."

Again, He called them hypocrites,
"Do you hear what you say?"
"If you knew your animal was thirsty
would you make it wait another day?
You say I shouldn't heal this woman,
because it's the Sabbath I should walk away."
There was silent humiliation
and the people loved Jesus more every day.

Luke 13:10-17

Overcoming Evil

The devil is far worse than the worst person
you will ever know.
Worse than the worst thing you could imagine,
he can make it so.
His role in the world is to keep you away from God
and His ways.
He uses every chance to turn you away from God every day.

No matter how good a person you are
he will always be there.
He will stop you from reaching your goal
by using your fear.
He will distort your vision until your path
is no longer clear.
And regardless of the path you take,
evil will always be there.

The devil has free reign in this world
but God is still in control.
Even when you fall
you can call Him
and He can save your soul.
Draw near to God and He will stay with you
and always keep you whole.
Overcoming evil, with faith in God,
should always be our goal.

Faith of Those Not Chosen

All she knew was she wanted her daughter back.
She couldn't bear to watch another demon attack.
Jesus works miracles but He's not here for her kind.
The lost sheep of Israel He came to find.

She heard He was entering into her region.
Just passing through, she had to get His attention.
She called "Son of David, have mercy on me!"
Nothing.
Her pain and affliction He didn't see.

"Son of David, have mercy on me" she cried out.
Again, He said nothing and continued about.
Those around Him said "She won't stop calling you.
"Should we send her away?
What should we do?"

She knelt before Him, "Help me"
and He began to say,
"Bread is for the children, it is not to be thrown away.
"It is not right to give to dogs what belongs to them".
And she said, "Even the dogs eat the crumbs left by men".

Her child was suffering from demon possession.
With all her courage she finally got His attention.
She'd be more grateful for crumbs than those with bread.
And at that moment her child was healed;
And the demon fled.

Matthew 15:21-28

At the Well

Before the nation was divided Jacob dug a well,
His twelve sons became the twelve tribes of Israel.
Now the land was separated, they could no longer agree.
Jesus entered enemy camp to set the captives free.

He waited at the well for her in the heat of the day,
Knowing she'd only come while others stayed away.
A spring of living water now sat on the well and waited,
For a broken woman whom He knew other women hated.

Here she came, clay pot in hand, to the well again.
Walking the same path every day on this day she met Him.
She had no problem talking to men
but still found herself caught off guard;
When Jesus asked her for a drink.
Her life had been so hard.

All her life she never felt that she was part of a team.
The devil knew the part she'd play
So he attacked her self-esteem.
Every time she lifted herself
he'd show up and beat her down;
He knew that through this woman
Jesus could save this town.

Always on the defensive she reminded him he was a Jew.
"I am a Samaritan Woman, we don't associate with you."
"Oh, if you knew the gift of God you would be asking me,"
"I would give you streams of living water and set you free."

She looked at the well he sat upon as she began to say,
"This well is deep and you have nothing
to draw with anyway.
"Are you better than our father Jacob
who gave us this well first?"
He said, "If you drink the water I give you,
you will never thirst."

In the middle of the night when no one else is there,
When your pain and loneliness are too much to bear,
There will be springs of living water welling up
into your soul,
To comfort you and give you back all the devil stole.

"Give me this water" she said,
"I don't want to come here anymore."
"Go home and get your husband, come back,
I'll tell you more."
"I have no husband", she replied,
and he confirmed that she was right.
"You've in fact been married to five
but not the one you had last night."

"I see that you're a prophet
but you don't worship as we do".
He said, "God is spirit so you must worship
in spirit and truth.
"A time will come when it will not matter
where you go to pray,
"Salvation is from the Jews;
your salvation has come today."

She said, "When the Messiah comes
He will explain it all to me."
Then Jesus declared,
"I, the one speaking to you, I am He."
When His disciples returned
she left her water jar and fled;
Back into town to tell the men all the things he'd said.

Jesus told His disciples
"It's time to reap where others have sown.
See the fields, the harvest is ripe
planted by hands not your own.
Others have done the work for you,
it is now your time to reap.
They thirst for truth the time has come
to gather up my sheep."

Many Samaritans were saved that day
because of this woman's story.
They went to Him and brought Him back
and got to see His glory.
They believed He was the savior;
He opened their eyes to see;
That He was the spring of living water
welling up to eternity.

John 4:4-26

It's You

It's you who made the sky so blue,
And filled it with stars at night.
Before any colors, before any light;
Before anything there was you.
And you made the sky so blue.

It's you who made the trees so tall,
And covered them with leaves of green.
Before any plants or colors were seen;
It was you before anything at all.
And you made the trees so tall.

It's you who made the sea so deep,
And filled it with life overflowing.
Before any water could start anything growing,
Before anyone could begin to reap,
It was you who made the fish in the sea so deep.

It's you who made the mountains so high;
Reaching up to the stars in your brilliant sky.
Before anyone could attempt to wonder why,
Before anyone could live or die,
It was you who made the mountains high.

It's you who made the sun so bright
To warm the planet earth down below.
Before anyone could begin to know.
It was you before there was any dark or light.
It was you before there was day or night.

It's you who made heaven and called it your home;
And filled it with angels to ever sing your praise.
Before any song, before any voice could be raised,
It was you, Father, in heaven sitting upon your thrown.
It's still you, Almighty Father, still calling us home.

Our Father's Voice

Quietly we wait and hope to hear our Father's voice.
To learn His will and obey;
it's us who've made that choice.
God only wants what's good for us;
He knows all of our needs.
So we are waiting to hear His word
and follow where it leads.

Prayerfully we wait for God to speak into our hearts.
Our faith grows stronger every day,
once the healing starts;
Until we find ourselves listening for His voice constantly;
And trusting that His word alone is what will set us free.

With open hearts, we invite the Holy Spirit of the one
Whom God has sent to be our friend,
His own begotten Son.
He gives to us His mercy and He frees us from our sin.
And the Holy Spirit within our hearts
brings us home again.

Life we've learned is better
when we seek God's Kingdom first;
And drink from the living water
that will satisfy our thirst.
It is His will we ask be done;
it's us who've made that choice.
So we ask in the name of Jesus,
let us hear Our Father's Voice.

A King

The spirit of God was upon Him,
Through Him prophesy was fulfilled.
God worked with Him and through Him,
And He did only as His father willed.

The miracles He performed made it clear,
And the people knew He was their king.
Those who ruled were filled with fear,
They knew their ruin He would bring.

He taught the people with love and mercy,
And revealed to them His father's love.
He told them what He was here to be,
That His Kingdom was from above.

Those in power He let take Him down,
He knew for this reason He was called.
With thorns they gave a king His crown,
To His own cross and death He crawled.

God sent His Son to take our place,
To endure the penalty of our sin.
He knew the agony He would face,
To bring His people back to Him.

God shook the earth when Jesus died,
The holy temple trembled with fear.
"He was the Son of God" the people cried.
To those who killed Him it was clear.

For our salvation He suffered and bled,
His precious blood wipes away our stains.
He rose from death to glory just as He said;
And now a king in Heaven He forever reigns.

Imagine John

Imagine for a moment, if you could.
Imagine. Humor me, if you would.
Imagine you're the closest one to the Lord.
Of all His apostles, you're the most adored.

Imagine, if you will, that you were at His side
When He turned water to wine for
the groom and his bride.
And all those at the wedding feast remarked that this wine
Was the finest of spirits to ever come from a vine.

Imagine that you're John, the beloved apostle, the one;
Who witnessed many miracles once they had begun.
Imagine you are with Him while He prays to God above;
A Son speaking to His Father with reverence and love.

Imagine being with the Lord day in and day out,
And learning firsthand what God's love is about.
And walking with Jesus sharing many special things.
Imagine being His favorite and the joy that this brings.

Imagine never leaving Him even when He faced His death.
Imagine Him speaking to you with His last dying breath.
Imagine the Book of Revelation being shown just to you.
Imagine sweet John and all the heavenly things he knew.

Imagine just for a moment, if you would dare to try,
Knowing that you'll be with Jesus on the very day you die.
Imagine you are the closest to being perfect in His eye.
Imagine John, the beloved apostle,
on whom God could rely.

Your Love Is My Reward

You fill my heart with joy and make that joy complete.
You help me to see the good in everyone I meet.
You help me find my prize even in defeat,
And you let me find the truth in the midst of deceit.

This world would like to hide you and all you represent.
Your followers hear your words and know what you meant;
When you spoke of sin and our ability to repent.
We know you and the Father and the reason you were sent.

The truth sustains me and helps me stay on course.
The evil one tempts me while feeling no remorse.
But I have you and your love to fight any evil force.
I draw from that power, and Jesus you're the source.

You fill my heart with joy and lead me every day.
Closer to your own heart which is where I long to stay.
I know your words
and know those words will never betray;
The faith I have in you, Lord, and the price you had to pay.

My heart is filled with gladness
because you are my Lord.
You help me in my fight for life;
you are my shield and sword.
Only goodness surrounds me.
My salvation is assured.
As long as I keep you in my heart
your love is my reward.

Seven More

Looking back he finds it amazing
how all these things played out,
And the difficult lesson to be learned
was learned without a doubt.
It all began with a single thought
until the thought took control,
And with every thought he found himself
falling deeper into a hole.

Every single action you take first
begins with a thought inside your head,
And whether that thought is good or bad
you're already being lead.
He knew about the love of God
and the direction he should take
But temptation was there every day
until he felt that he might break.

The enticement was there for the taking,
the attraction was so strong.
His world was black and white, no gray,
and he knew right from wrong.
With everything he had he fought
until the thought was finally gone,
And with a sense of relief he felt he was free
and started to move on.
It was then that he heard the voices,
they were screaming inside his head.
What he thought he had overcome
had become his biggest dread.

The temptation was different this time,
it was stronger than before
The evil thought he fought had left
but returned with seven more.
He found himself in a place he hated
and only sadness was his friend.
He was bound by Satan
who brought other demons to bring him to his end.

They allowed no thoughts that could lift him
only his suffering was for real.
They pulled him further away from God,
His love and mercy he could not feel.

It took everything he had to find the truth,
he knew the truth would set him free.
Somehow, he found himself back in God's grace,
nowhere else he'd rather be.
Through the pain he learned that
when temptation enters as it always will,
You must stay strong
knowing that you will need to be stronger still.

Evil will return when you cast him out
and bring with him seven more.
The strength of this war against your spirit
is greater than the one before.
Call on the angels of God and His Word
to strengthen your soul.
They will bring your prayers to God;
He will rescue you and make you whole.

God So Loved The World

God so loved the world,
That He sent His only Son.
He suffered and died for our sin,
And our victory was won.

God so loved the world,
He raised His Son from the dead;
So we might have life through Him,
By the innocent blood He shed.

God so loved the world,
Even though it was depraved.
Those who love His Son
Are those who will be saved.

In The Comfort of My Shepherd

A baby knows her mother's voice,
it's one of the first sounds she'll hear.
She listens for it and feels safe
every time that voice draws near.
It reassures her, comforts her,
tells her there is nothing to fear.
She listens for no other voice,
only her mother's voice is clear.

More than a mother, Jesus says,
I will fight to the death for you.
You are my own, my beloved,
for you there's nothing I won't do.
I will never leave your side
no matter what you're going through.
I will give you everything you need
to live a life that's rich and true.

You will hear other voices
but what they're saying won't be real,
Their purpose is to hurt you,
your joy they'll try to steal.
Don't let others rob you
of what only I can make you feel.
I am the gate, many are my own,
and those who enter I will heal.

I will watch and protect them from attack,
always keep them in my sight.
I will let them roam freely
in good pastures and always be their guide.
They will find me every time they look,
from my own I'll never hide.
If you hear me, you hear my Father,
and you'll never be denied.

My Prayer

Oh, my Father in Heaven with my Jesus by your side,
Great and holy is your name;
In your love I will abide.

Your Kingdom is all around me
your great Kingdom is so near.
I can see you in all creation;
In every sound your name I hear.

Father in Heaven, where your perfect will is done,
Let your will be all I know,
let your will and mine be one.

Fill my soul every day with every good thing that I need.
Fill me to overflowing with a heart that knows no greed.

Help me forgive others so that mercy comes back to me.
For with the measure I use, the same measure I will see.

Keep me from temptation, help keep me far from sin.
Rescue me from every evil so this race I can win.

Only you have the power,
with my Jesus and all His glory.
For you are the Kingdom;
Where I always long to be.
Amen.

Walk With You

Lost in my own head, thoughts scattered all about.
Remembering the things you said, not having a doubt;
That you are here with me every step of the way.
Everything I do you see; you hear everything I say.

Everything that's said to me is clearly heard by you.
From these lies set me free to only hear what's true.
Help me see what's real as if looking through your eyes.
Help me only feel the things that let me grow inside.

You are with me always. Please don't put me down.
I see every one of my days as I look along the ground.
There you are; just as you said, I'm cradled in your hand.
Through this dread I only see your footprints in the sand.

I trust in you and your love for me and all that is true.
I know that you are here for me to help me follow through.
Give me the strength I need to walk with you side by side.
Keep me strong in thought and deed
and always be my guide.

Humbled Publican

In their self-righteousness
some came to oppose this Jesus.
They said He walked with us,
yet he chose to stay with Zacchaeus.
Our Messiah was promised to Abraham
His mercy frees us.
We have kept traditions. We follow the law.
Why doesn't He see us?

Jesus knew their hearts were hard,
and so He told them this story;
About a Pharisee who thought,
"I'm perfect, I have no need to worry".
He entered the temple, walked right in
and said "Lord I thank thee
"That I am not a sinner,
there's nothing you need to do for me".

And then the Publican who dared not enter,
he knew of his sin.
He beat his breast
unable to lift even his eyes to Heaven.
He cried "Be merciful to me a sinner.
Where do I begin".
He knew he would never find salvation from within.

The Pharisee trusted in himself
that he would be saved for sure.
The Publican knew he had to change,
not be the man he was before.
The Pharisee exalted himself;
the Publican knew his spirit was poor.
He left justified.
Not the Pharisee,
Who was sure he deserved more.

Luke 18:9-14
Luke 19:1-7

Into the Kingdom

Wearing the finest linens
and walking with a certain authority,
He approached Jesus, calling him
Good Teacher, he said "Tell me,
How do I inherit eternal life?
What must I do to be free?"
Jesus said, "Only God is good; why speak that way to me?"

"You know the commandments
thou shall not commit adultery,
Thou shall not steal, or murder or give false testimony
And if you honor your father and mother
you'll see God's glory."
Encouraged he said, "Since I was a boy I have kept all these."

Jesus said "One more thing,
you must sell everything you own,
If you follow me, you will want for nothing,
you'll never be alone.

And your treasure in Heaven
will outweigh anything you've known."
Grieving, he knew his wealth would
keep him from God's throne.

The others said, "Not one of us can be saved
no matter what we do."
Jesus explained, "Heaven's not something
you can buy your way into,
It's difficult for the rich to share their riches
and enter it's true.
It's like holding the eye of a needle
and asking a camel to walk through."

"Then who can be saved?" they asked,
"for us there's surely no way."
They were well aware of all the commandments
they didn't obey.
Jesus said, "God knew it was impossible,
man would always stray,
God's grace will allow you into the kingdom.
There is no other way."

Matthew 19:16-26

Speak Into My Heart, Oh Lord

Speak into my heart, oh Lord,
Show me all your ways,
Protect me all my days,
Keep me in your gaze.

Speak into my heart, oh Lord,
Show me how to live,
Help me to forgive,
Forgive the things I did.

Speak into my heart, oh Lord,
Show me what to say,
Keep the evil one away,
Hear me when I pray.

Speak into my heart, oh Lord,
Show me all your ways,
Help me through this maze,
Stay with me always.

Speak into my heart, oh Lord,
I know that you're the one
Who made the moon and sun
And me and everyone.

Speak into my heart, oh Lord,
Show me what to do
To show others it is true
That we can rely on you.

Speak into my heart, oh Lord,
Let me work for you,
Show me what to do,
To show others it is true
That our only hope is you.

Power and Faith

By this time God's people were oppressed
under Roman rule.
Rome was the thrown and Israel it's footstool.
They didn't know who God was,
they were ruthless and cruel.
God's people were losing hope in a Messiah to overrule.

God sent His only Son
who was now a man with power and might.
He came with a message of hope
and mercy for the Israelites.
He forgave their sins so with their God they could reunite.
Miracles were worked through Him,
He was the truth and light.

A Roman Centurion had a servant
whom he cared deeply about,
At the point of death, he thought
this servant I can't do without.
He heard about Jesus and thought
He could save him, no doubt.
So he sent the Elders of the Jews
thinking they'd have more clout.

They were not far from his home
when he sent friends to say,
"Lord, don't trouble yourself,
I'm not worthy, be on your way.
"You see I too have authority and soldiers
at my command every day,
"I tell this one come or this one go, or order them to stay."

By now there was a crowd
and Jesus turned to them and said,
The religious leaders were with me
when they saw 5,000 fed,
And still they are hypocrites whose faith is dead,
They show my people no mercy but condemnation instead.

This Centurion speaks truth,
he understands who I am.
He knows the authority I was given
before time began.
Yet my own people have become blind
to my father's plan.
This servant has been saved
through the faith of this man.

Luke 7:1-10

Your Love

Come let me feel the warmth of your true love beside me.
From all evil and wickedness and sickness please hide me.
Along the path to your kingdom I pray you will guide me.
I was once bound by Satan but your love has untied me.

My faith in your love, I believe is what saved me,
And the more my faith grew the more Satan craved me.
With every victory over temptation
my heart aches to praise thee.
Still with all I've been shown
your love will always amaze me.

Come let me feel your love that you give so freely.
By the power of your love you were able to free me.
God make me good in your eyes
so that my eyes may see thee
In your kingdom with your true love for all of eternity.

Call Out

His disciples left their homes, their jobs, their families
To follow Jesus now coming to the end of His ministry.
Along the way to Jerusalem He told of His agony.
He walked slowly through Jericho on His way to destiny.

What He had come into the world to do
was now almost complete.
People on their way to Passover now lined the street.
This Jesus who performed miracles they came out to greet.
This would be the last time they'd have the chance to meet.

A blind man named Bartimaeus begged here every day.
He took his cup and his beggar's coat
knowing people walked that way.
He survived by mercy filling his cup,
but blind he would stay,
Until now; and he was shouting
"Jesus!" from where he lay.

Those around him told him to stop
but he cried out even more.
Jesus walked on; His mind fixed
on what God had sent Him for.
Until He heard, "Son of David!"
something He could not ignore.
They said "Cheer up! On your feet!
It's you He's asking for."

When he called Him "Son of David" he was saying he knew,
That He was the Messiah
and what he'd heard of Him was true.
Jesus asked the blind man,
"What is it you would like me to do?"
"I want to see" and Jesus said,
"Go, your faith has healed you".

We must call out leaving whatever we need to leave behind.
Bartimaeus threw his coat aside
and followed Jesus, no longer blind.
Then He told His disciples
"Go into the village
and there you will find
a colt; bring it.
I will need it to finish the work I've been assigned."

Mark 10:46-52

We, Like Moses

Like Moses, we are called to greatness
to set God's people free.
A baby left in the river became
part of Pharaoh's family.
His anger forced him into hiding
keeping him from what would be.
Years went by but God will always
come looking for you and me.

He knows where each of us is
but saying it out loud is the key.
We are like Adam who hid from God,
after eating from the tree.
God asked, "Where are you?"
knowing he had met the enemy.
He said, "I was naked and afraid."
And fear became a reality.

Fear was in Moses when he told God,
"I have no authority.
"These people have been beaten, forced into slavery.
"They have no hope,
what makes you think that they'll listen to me?"
He had no faith in himself
but God would open his eyes to see.

He asked Moses,
"What is it you are holding in your hand?"
Moses answered, "It's a rod."
God said, "Throw it on the sand".
It became a serpent and being afraid,
Moses turned and ran.
He had everything he needed to fulfill God's plan.

"Moses! Take the serpent by the tail!" God said.
The very things that we are running from,
God makes us face instead.
The things we fear the most
are those things inside our head.
They are put there by the enemy so that we can be misled.

Moses did as God commanded and again he held a rod.
Seeing his power his mission no longer seemed so odd.
We, like Moses, have the power to save,
to walk where angels trod.
The power Moses believed he had saved the people of God.

Exodus 4:1-5

Epilogue

God is waiting for each of us to call on Him. He stands at each of our doors waiting to be invited in. When you let Him in, your life will no longer be the same. Ask and you shall receive is so simple; we complicate it.

It is very important to God that we ask. When Jesus was passing through a village and the blind man named Bartmaeus heard the people shouting to Jesus he too shouted "Son of David, have mercy on me". He went to the blind man and asked, "What is it you would like me to do for you?" It seemed obvious, he was blind. And he answered, "Please Lord I want to see." Not only was his sight restored immediately but he got to see the Glory of God.

The good news is that we don't have to become anything, we don't have to be perfect. He found those that had no chance on their own, those looked down upon, some of the greatest sinners, and turned their lives around. Because they were given so much and forgiven so much they became His best followers.

Too many of us live in the memory of past disappointments and mistakes. They almost become who we are if we allow them too. Everyone makes mistakes and everyone has regrets. That's when we have to turn to the promises God made, that He would be there for us if we seek Him and honor Him.

When we honor God, it allows Him to go to work and He shows us what we need to let go of and what we need to hold on to. When we listen then we can learn and let go of the memory and the pain it brings. This is when we have to take control of our thoughts and replace them with thoughts of God and His promises.

I have no problem talking about God; somehow He gets worked into my conversation. Father Walsh told me I was a living gospel and I loved that compliment. Jesus sent His apostles out to preach just as they had seen Him preach and they performed miracles just as Jesus had. That's what we're here for, as soldiers, to strengthen and lift each other. I use the gift God gave me through my books and talk about Him to all those who will listen.

I had my only daughter, Brooke, late in life and I was in awe of everything. While I was pregnant, I would make the sign of the cross on my ever-growing belly every day and ask God to make her happy and healthy in body and mind. There is more power in the sign of the cross than we understand. She is now attending college and she is the most wonderful person I could have hoped for. Beautiful inside and out.

One day when she was very young I asked her out of the blue, "Where were you all the while Mommy was waiting for you?" I wasn't really looking for an answer but I heard this little voice say, "I was with Jesus." I asked, "And how did you come to be with Mommy?" and she answered, "I went to talk to Jesus, I said I really want a mommy; I blinked my eyes and saw all angels, I blinked my eyes and saw all clouds, I blinked my eyes and saw Mother Mary then I blinked my eyes and I saw you". I never talked of Mary and she wasn't old enough to want to impress me. That seed was planted in her by my prayer, by the sign of the cross before she was born.

We are planting seeds all the time with every thought we dwell on, every word we say out loud, every prayer we pray and every Bible passage we read. The life we're living right now was manifested by the thoughts we had and the things we said years ago. Our thoughts, words and actions are seeds we plant and we can only expect to grow more of the same. An apple seed will produce another apple tree.

It is important that we have a grateful heart. Being grateful will bring more things to us that will make us grateful. Jesus found those who needed His mercy most and He showed them mercy and their hearts were the most grateful. He would go out of His way to find them, call them out of trees by name, as he did with Zacchaeus.

These Gospel-inspired poems speak of those stories told of God and by God. I am grateful for the opportunity to bring this message to you. I hope it keeps you close to God or helps you to know God and how powerful He is and what He wants to do for us.

Jesus lived among us to show us who God is and how we should live to receive the life He wants to give us. A life in abundance with joy and love. Jesus showed us how, through Him, we could recieve salvation.

Take time each day; tell Him how important He is to you, thank Him for His love and mercy. He will never forsake us. We are His beloved.

Order Information

REDEMPTION
PRESS

To order additional copies of this book, please visit
www.redemption-press.com.
Also available on Amazon.com and BarnesandNoble.com
Or by calling toll free 1-844-2REDEEM.